Contents

OXFORD
UNIVERSITY PRESS

Great Clarendon Street, Oxford, OX2 6DP, United Kingdom

Oxford University Press is a department of the University
of Oxford. It furthers the University's objective of excellence
in research, scholarship, and education by publishing
worldwide. Oxford is a registered trade mark of Oxford
University Press in the UK and in certain other countries

British Library Cataloguing in Publication Data
Data available

ISBN: 978-0-19-276477-5

10 9 8 7 6 5 4

Paper used in the production of this book is a natural, recyclable product
made from wood grown in sustainable forests. The manufacturing process
conforms to the environmental regulations of the country of origin.

Printed and bound in Great Britain by Bell and Bain Ltd, Glasgow

Acknowledgements

Series Editor: Clare Kirtley

Cover illustration by Barbara Vagnozzi

Miss, Miss! illustrated by Ross Collins

Singing Dad illustrated by Barbara Vagnozzi

Doctor Duck illustrated by Deborah Allwright

Mr Zed illustrated by Anni Axworthy

The Odd Pet

Tips for reading The Odd Pet together

This story practises these sounds:

s m c t g p a o r l d b
f h i u v y z j n k e

Ask your child to point to these letters and say the sounds (e.g. *k* as in *kit*, not the letter name *kay*). Look out for these letters in the story.

Your child might find these words tricky:

have now of the

These words are common, but your child may not have learned how to sound them out yet. Say the words for your child if they do not know them.

Before you begin, ask your child to read the title by sounding out first (saying each letter out loud, e.g. *p-e-t*) and then blending the word together (e.g. *pet*), as much as possible. Look at the picture together. What do you think this story is about?

Remind your child to read unfamiliar words by saying the individual sounds and then blending them together quickly to read the word. When you have finished reading the story, look through it again and:

- Ask your child, *How did Kim and Jim get a zog?* (Viv gave them one of the zogs that hatched from her zog's eggs)
- Find two words that rhyme on the first page of the story (*Kim, Jim*). Ask your child to say the middle sound in these words. Find and read some more words with the *i* sound in the middle (*Viv, sit*). Try to write some of the words. Say all of the sounds in the word separately then write the letter that makes each sound.

Kim has a cat. Jim has a dog.

But Viv has an odd pet.

It is a zog! Not a cat, not a dog, but a zog!

The zog is fat. It has ten red legs.

It can run and hop.

It can sit and beg.

The zog has lots of eggs!

The zog sits on the eggs.
It sits and sits.

Tap, tap, tap!
Tap, tap, tap!

Lots of zogs!

17

Now Kim has a cat and a zog.

Jim has a dog and a zog.

Feb
28

And Viv has ten zogs!

Miss, Miss!

Tips for reading Miss, Miss! together

This story practises these letter patterns:

ll ss ff zz

Ask your child to point to these letter patterns and say the sounds (e.g. *ll* as in *full*). Look out for these letter patterns in the story.

Your child might find these words tricky:

ball I my the

These words are common, but your child may not have learned how to sound them out yet. Say the words for your child if they do not know them.

Before you begin, ask your child to read the title by sounding out first (saying each sound out loud, e.g. *m-i-ss*) and then blending the word together (e.g. *miss*). Look at the picture together. What do you think this story is about?

Remind your child to read unfamiliar words by saying the individual sounds and then blending them together quickly to read the word. When you have finished reading the story, look through it again and:

- Talk about what Miss Hill might be thinking on the last page of the story.

- Find and read words in the story that end with the sound *s* (*Miss, Tess, mess, yes, gets, bus, Ross*). Notice that the sound *s* is written in two ways (*s, ss*). Find more letter patterns on page 37 where one sound is written with two letters (*zz* in *buzz*, *ff* in *off*, *ss* in *Ross*).

23

25

31

Miss Hill gets on the bus.

Miss Hill gets off the bus.

38

This and That

Tips for reading This and That together

This story practises these letter patterns:

sh ch th

Ask your child to point to these letter patterns and say the sounds (e.g. *th* as in *thumb*). Look out for these letter patterns in the story.

Your child might find these words tricky:

have Mr Mrs some

These words are common, but your child may not have learned how to sound them out yet. Say the words for your child if they do not know them.

Before you begin, ask your child to read the title by sounding out first (saying each sound out loud, e.g. *th-i-s*) and then blending the word together (e.g. *this*) as much as possible. Look at the picture together. What do you think this story is about?

Remind your child to read unfamiliar words by saying the individual sounds and then blending them together quickly to read the word. When you have finished reading the story, look through it again and:

- Ask your child, *How did Tim make his rabbit?*
- Find the words that begin with the *sh* sound (*shop, shell, ship*). Ask your child to point to the letter pattern that makes the beginning sound of the words (*sh*). Have fun thinking of some more words that contain the *sh* sound (*push, cash, shed, rush, dish*).

This is Mr Chan's shop.

Mr Chan sells pens, pads and maps.

Tim is in Mr Chan's shop.

44

This is Miss Thin's shop.

Miss Thin sells eggs, nuts and carrots.

Tim is in Miss Thin's shop.

49

This is Mrs Ship's shop.

51

Mrs Ship sells jugs, shells and chess sets.

Tim is in Mrs Ship's shop.

This is Tim's rabbit!

Fish and Chips

Tips for reading Fish and Chips together

This story practises these letter patterns:

sh   ch   th   wh

Ask your child to point to these letter patterns and say the sounds (e.g. *ch* as in *chat*). Look out for these letter patterns in the story.

Your child might find these words tricky:

come   I'm   my   too

These words are common, but your child may not have learned how to sound them out yet. Say the words for your child if they do not know them.

Before you begin, ask your child to read the title by sounding out first (saying each sound out loud, e.g. *f-i-sh*) and then blending the word together (e.g. *fish*), as much as possible. Look at the picture together. What do you think this story is about?

Remind your child to read unfamiliar words by saying the individual sounds and then blending them together quickly to read the word. When you have finished reading the story, look through it again and:

- Talk about how Ron Rabbit felt at the end of the story and why (he was exhausted because the shop was very busy).

- Find words that begin or end with the *ch* sound (*chip, which, much*). Ask your child to point to the letter pattern that makes this sound (*ch*). Have fun thinking of some more words that contain the *ch* sound (*chin, chill, rich, such*).

This is Ron Rabbit.

Ron has a job in a fish and chip shop.

69

Singing Dad

Tips for reading Singing Dad together

This story practises these letter patterns:

ng   ll   ff   sh   ch   th

Ask your child to point to these letter patterns and say the sounds (e.g. *ng* as in *ring*). Look out for these letter patterns in the story.

Your child might find these words tricky:

after   all   day   he   I'm   never
she   singer   the   to

These words are common, but your child may not have learned how to sound them out yet. Say the words for your child if they do not know them.

Before you begin, ask your child to read the title by sounding out first (saying each letter out loud, e.g. *d-a-d*) and then blending the word together (e.g. *dad*). Look at the picture together. What do you think this story is about?

Remind your child to read unfamiliar words by saying the individual sounds and then blending them together quickly to read the word. When you have finished reading the story, look through it again and:

- Ask your child, *Why did Mum tell Dad off?*

- Find some words that contain the *ng* sound (*sings, long, song, fishing, digging, chopping*). Ask your child to point to the letter pattern that makes this sound (*ng*). Have fun thinking of some words that rhyme with *sing (thing, king, ring, wing).*

Dad is a singer.

He sings all day long.

Song, after song,

after song, after song!

He sings to the cat and
he sings to the dog.

He sings in the sun

and he sings in the fog.

He sings in the shops

and he sings in the shed.

He sings in the bus

and he sings in his bed.

He sings when he's fishing.

He sings when he jogs.

He sings when he's digging

and chopping up logs.

Mum tells Dad off.
"I'm fed up with that song."

Mum *never* sings . . .

but she *hums* all day long!

Doctor Duck

Tips for reading Doctor Duck together

This story practises these letter patterns:

ng   ck   x   qu

Ask your child to point to these letter patterns and say the sounds (e.g. *qu* as in *queen*). Look out for these letter patterns in the story.

Your child might find these words tricky:

he   I   of   said   she   some   to
was   came   come   days   doctor

These words are common, but your child may not have learned how to sound them out yet. Say the words for your child if they do not know them.

Before you begin, ask your child to read the title by sounding out first (saying each sound out loud, e.g. *d-u-ck*) and then blending the word together (e.g. *duck*), as much as possible. Look at the picture together. What do you think this story is about?

Remind your child to read unfamiliar words by saying the individual sounds and then blending them together quickly to read the word. When you have finished reading the story, look through it again and:

- Ask your child, *Why did Mum ask the doctor to come quick?*

- Find some words that contain the letter pattern *qu* (*quick, quack*). Find and read some words in the book which end with the sound *k* (*duck, sick, quick, quack, luck, back, milk, yuk*). Say what letter patterns make the *k* sound at the end of these words (*ck, k*). What other letter can make the *k* sound (*c*)?

Bob Bug was in his cot.

"Get up, Bob," said Dad.

But Bob did not get up.
"I am hot!" he said.

"Bob is sick!" said Mum. "Quick! I will ring Doctor Duck."

"Mum is a fusspot," said Dad.

Mum Bug rang Doctor Duck.

"Come quick!" she said. "Bob is sick!"

"Quack, quack!" said Doctor Duck.
He got his box of pills.

"I will mix this pill up with some milk," he said.

"Sip this," said Doctor Duck to Bob Bug.

"Yuk," said Bob, but he had a sip.

"Quack, quack!" said
Doctor Duck.

"I will come back in six days."

When Doctor Duck came back,
Bob was hopping and singing.

But Dad Bug was in bed.
"I am hot! I am sick!" he said.

"Bad luck, Dad," said Mum.
"Dad is a fusspot!" said Bob.

Mr Zed

Tips for reading Mr Zed together

This story practises these letter patterns:

ll ff zz sh th ng ck
x qu wh

Ask your child to point to these letter patterns and say the sounds (e.g. *wh* as in *which*). Look out for these letter patterns in the story.

Your child might find these words tricky:

he of says she Mr no
gives the to was be

These words are common, but your child may not have learned how to sound them out yet. Say the words for your child if they do not know them.

Before you begin, ask your child read the title by sounding out first (saying each letter out loud, e.g. *Z-e-d*) and then blending the word together (e.g. *Zed*), as much as possible. Look at the picture together. What do you think this story is about?

Remind your child to read unfamiliar words by saying the individual sounds and then blending them together quickly to read the word. When you have finished reading the story, look through it again and:

- Ask your child, *Can you remember what comes out of Mr Zed's hat?* (puppet, mug, quill, pen, ten rabbits)

- Find the words that end with the letter pattern *ck* (Patrick, tick, tack, tock). Try to write the word *tock*. Say all the sounds in the word (*t-o-ck*) then write the letter patterns that make each sound.

Patrick is six. He is having fun with Jeff, Ellen and Wong-Jin.

Lots of singing and puffing!

Lots of whizzing! Lots of kicking and yelling!

Then Mum says, "Hush!"
She beckons them in.

"This is Mr Zed," says Mum.

"Sit on the rug!" says Mr Zed.

Mr Zed has a top hat.
"A rabbit is in it!" says Patrick.

Mr Zed taps the hat.
"Tick tack tock!" he says.

"It's a rabbit!" yells Patrick.
But is it?

No, it's a puppet. Mr Zed gives the
puppet to Ellen.

Then he taps the hat.
"Tick tack tock!"

"It's a rabbit!" yells Jeff.
But is it?

No, it's a mug. Mr Zed gives
it to Jeff.

Then he taps his hat.
"Tick tack tock."

"It's a rabbit!" yells Wong-Jin.
But is it?

No, it's a quill pen. Mr Zed gives it to Wong-Jin.

"I wish it was a rabbit," says Patrick. "Can I tap the hat?"

Patrick taps the hat and says, "Tick tack tock." Will it be a rabbit?

No, it's ten rabbits!